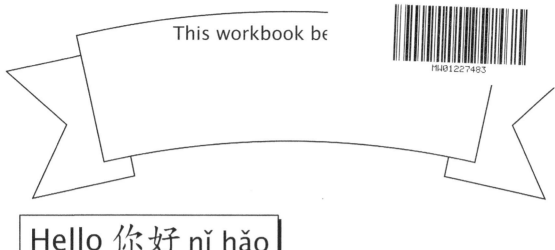

This workbook be

MW01227483

Hello 你好 nǐ hǎo

This workbook introduces basic words for family members and pets as Chinese characters with practice writing pages. Use pencils, color pencils, crayons and pens to write, color, draw as well as solve fun puzzles. Learn to write Chinese with creative, logic and reasoning activities. Pinyin, English translations and pictures are used to describe the characters.

Write at least two pages twice a week. Ask your child to think about the pronounciation, meaning and stroke order of each character while writing. Your child can check the stars at the top corner of each page to show how well he/she thought they did.

Trace over the gray characters by following the correct numbered stroke order as shown for the first few grids. Do not worry about the thickness of the gray lines. Use a pencil or pen to trace down the middle of the gray lines. Practice with the 2 sample grids below.

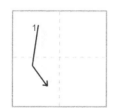 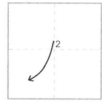

Thank you for choosing **Chinese For Kids My Family Workbook Ages 5+ (Simplified)**. Free Mandarin audio clips and worksheets are available on www.adoreneko.com. Have fun writing and learning!

Chinese For Kids My Family Workbook Ages 5+ (Simplified)
ISBN: 978-1721771707

© 2018 Queenie Law
Adore Neko Designs (www.adoreneko.com)

Let's Practice Writing

I, me
wǒ

我

我

Color

Color the picture and the Chinese character 我 (I, me).

🐟 Trace and write the Chinese character 我 (I, me).

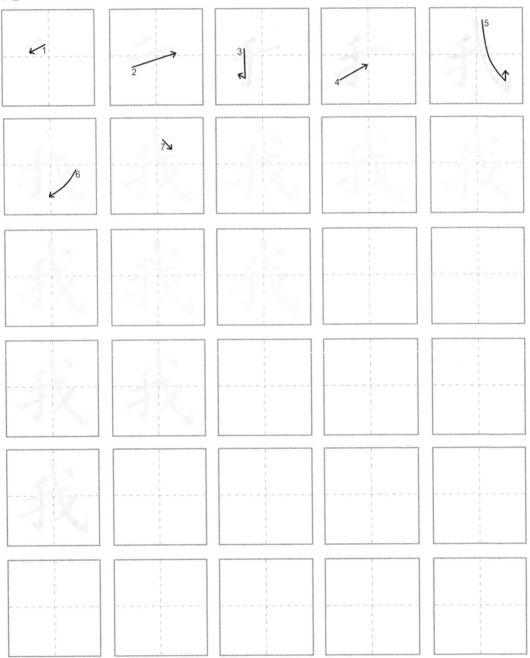

Let's Practice Writing

Trace and Draw

Trace the picture frame below. Draw a picture of you inside the frame.

Trace and write the Chinese character 我 (I, me).

I, me
wǒ

Let's Practice Writing

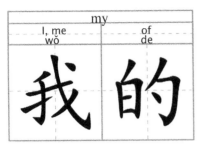

my	
I, me wǒ	of de

Helpful Tip

When 我 and 的 are put together, they form the word 我的 meaning "my".

Trace and write the Chinese character 的 (of).

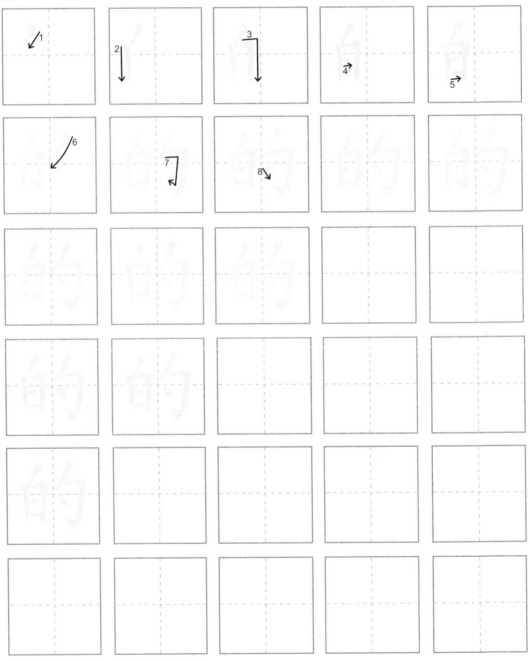

4

Let's Practice Writing

Maze

Start from the arrow at 我 (I, me) and draw a line to 的 (of) to make the word 我的 (my).

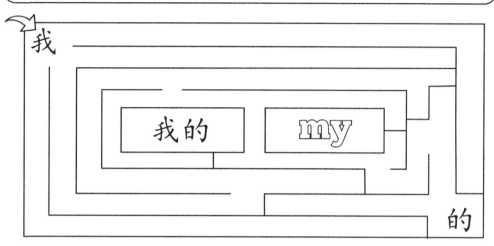

Trace and write the Chinese character 我的 (my).

my	
I, me wǒ	of de

5

family, home
jiā

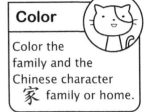

🐚 Trace and write the Chinese character 家 (family, home).

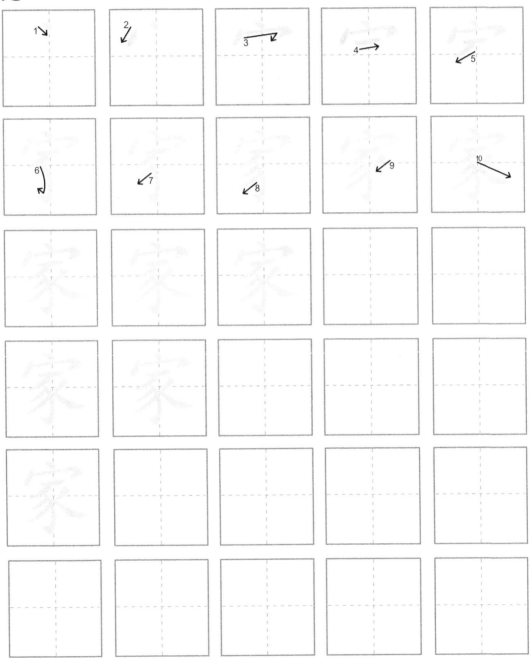

Let's Practice Writing

Draw

Draw your 家 family and home in the box below.

○ Trace and write the Chinese character 家 (family, home).

family, home
jiā

Let's Practice Writing

family member	
family, home jiā	person rén
家	人

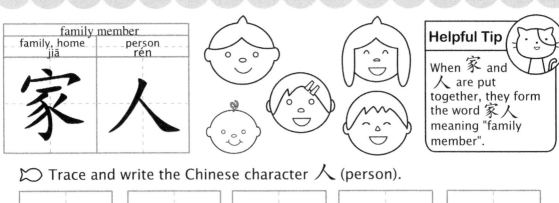

Helpful Tip

When 家 and 人 are put together, they form the word 家人 meaning "family member".

Trace and write the Chinese character 人 (person).

Let's Practice Writing

Match

Draw a line from each 人 (person) to the matching shape.

Trace and write the Chinese character 家人 (family member).

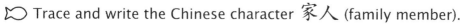

family member	
family, home jiā	person rén

Let's Practice Writing

grandpa (dad's father) yé
爷

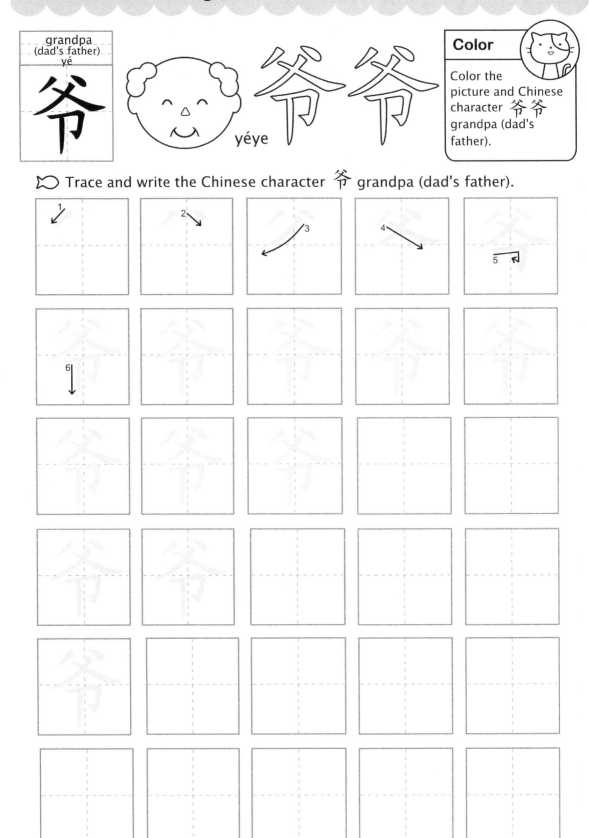

yéye

Color

Color the picture and Chinese character 爷爷 grandpa (dad's father).

Trace and write the Chinese character 爷 grandpa (dad's father).

Let's Practice Writing

Maze

Draw a line from the 爷爷 grandpa (dad's father) to the heart.

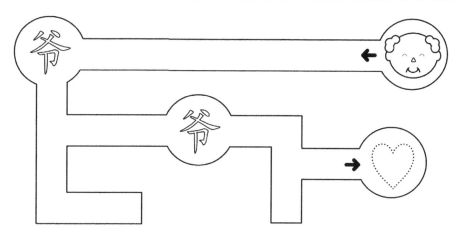

Trace and write the Chinese character 爷 grandpa (dad's father).

grandpa
(dad's father)
yé

Let's Practice Writing

grandma
(dad's mother)
nǎi

奶

nǎinai

Color

Color the picture and Chinese characters 奶奶 grandma (dad's mother).

Trace and write the Chinese character 奶 grandma (dad's mother).

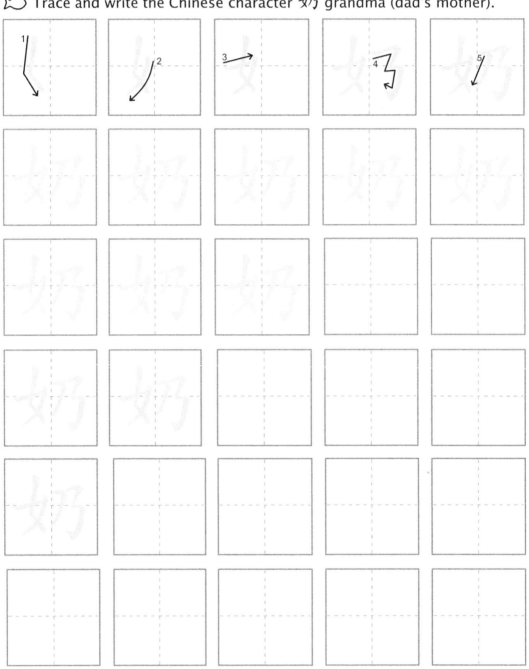

Let's Practice Writing

Maze

Draw a line from the 奶奶 grandma (dad's mother) to the heart.

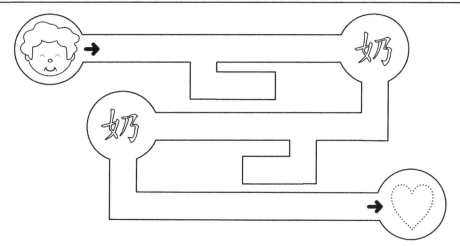

🐟 Trace and write the Chinese character 奶 grandma (dad's mother).

grandma (dad's mother) nǎi				

Let's Practice Writing

grandpa (mom's father)	
outside	husband's dad
wài	gōng
外	公

🐟 Trace and write the Chinese character 外 (outside).

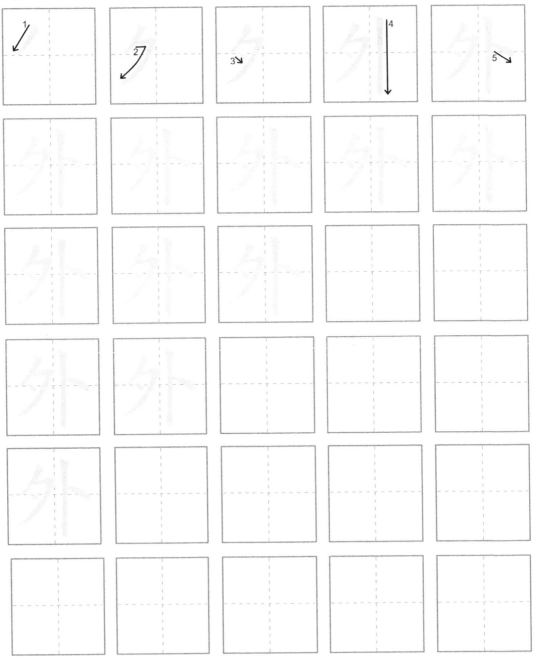

Let's Practice Writing

grandpa (mom's father)	
outside wài	husband's dad gōng
外	公

外公

wài gōng

Color

Color the picture and Chinese characters 外公 grandpa (mom's father).

🐟 Trace and write the Chinese character 公 (husband's father).

Let's Practice Writing

Compare

Compare the 外公 grandpa's (mom's father's) face in the left example to the faces on the right. Circle the differences.

Trace and write the Chinese character 外公 grandpa (mom's father).

grandpa (mom's father)	
outside wài	husband's dad gōng

Let's Practice Writing

grandma (mom's mother)	
outside wài	husband's mom pó
外	婆

外婆

wài pó

Trace and write the Chinese character 婆 husband's mom.

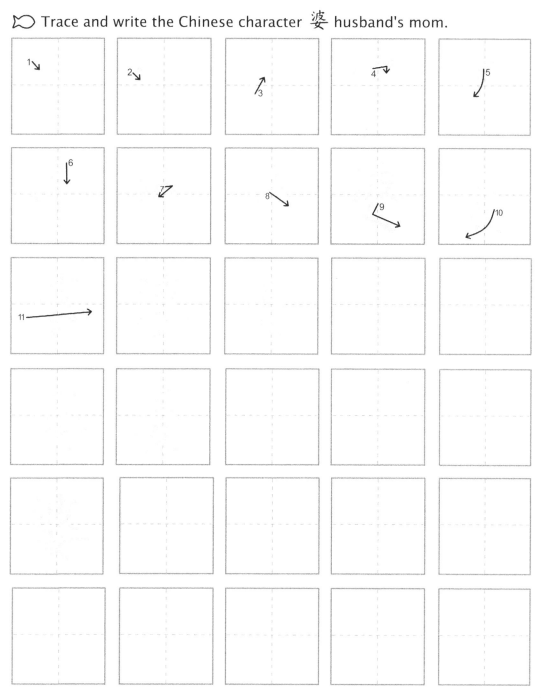

Let's Practice Writing

Compare

Compare the 外婆 grandma's (mom's mother's) face on the left example to the faces on the right. Circle the differences.

Example

Trace and write the Chinese character 外婆 grandma (mom's mother).

grandma (mom's mother)	
outside	husband's mom
wài	pó
外	婆

Let's Practice Writing

🐟 Trace and write the Chinese characters.

grandpa (mom's father)	
outside wài	husband's dad gōng

grandma (mom's mother)	
outside wài	husband's mom pó

Let's Practice Writing

dad
bà

爸

bàba

Color

Color the picture and Chinese characters 爸爸 dad.

🐟 Trace and write the Chinese character 爸 (dad).

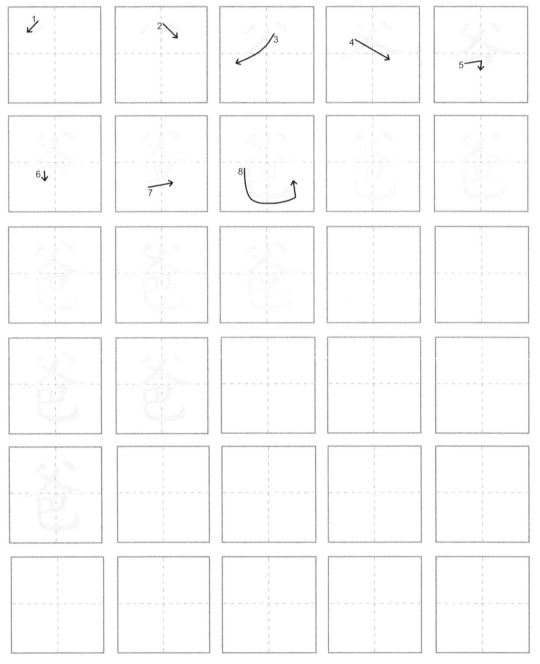

Let's Practice Writing

Find

Look at the two rows of words for dad. Circle the set of 爸爸 that is not like the others in each row.

Trace and write the Chinese character 爸 (dad).

dad				
bà				

mom
mā

妈

mmāma

Color

Color the picture and Chinese characters 妈妈 (mom).

🐟 Trace and write the Chinese character 妈 (mom).

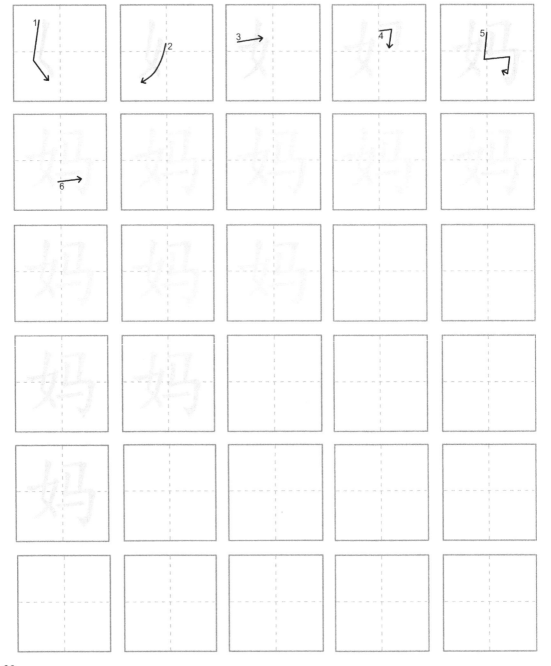

Let's Practice Writing

 Analogy

Look at the example. Circle the box with 妈 that should go where the question mark is.

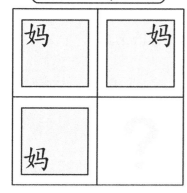

Example

Trace and write the Chinese character 妈 (mom).

mom				
mā				

Let's Practice Writing

older brother
gē
哥

gēgē

Color

Color the picture and Chinese characters 哥哥 (older brother).

🐟 Trace and write the Chinese character 哥 (older brother).

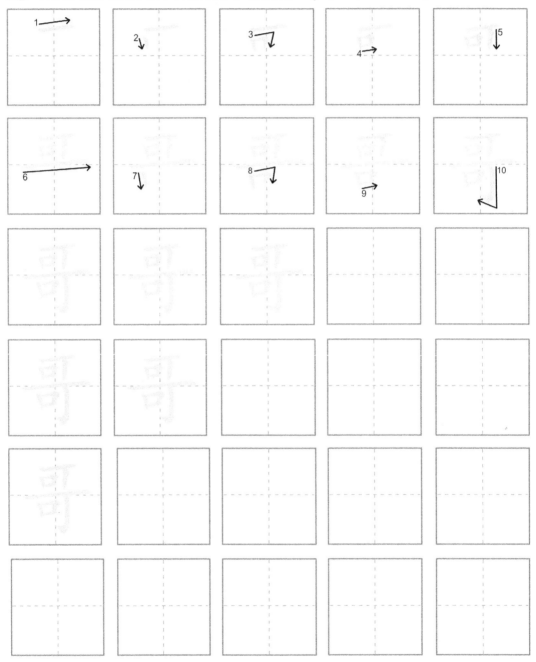

Let's Practice Writing

Trace

Trace a path along the dashed lines from the picture of the older brother to the Chinese character 哥.

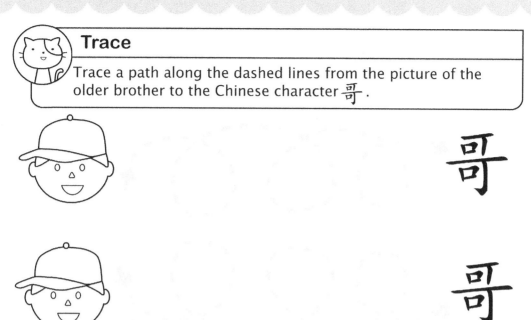

🐟 Trace and write the Chinese character 哥 (older brother).

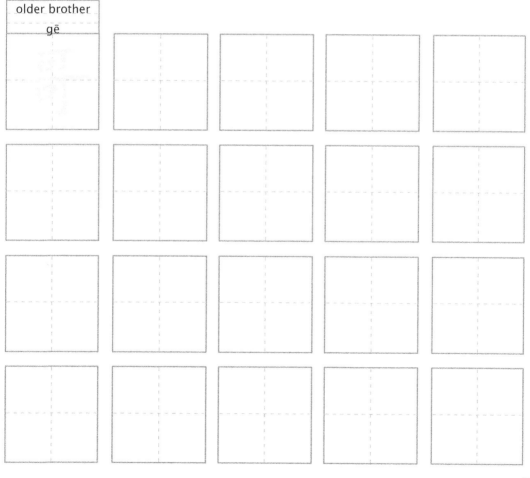

Let's Practice Writing

★ ★ ★

older sister
jiě
姐

jiějiě

Color

Color the picture and Chinese characters 姐姐 (older sister).

🐟 Trace and write the Chinese character 姐 (older sister).

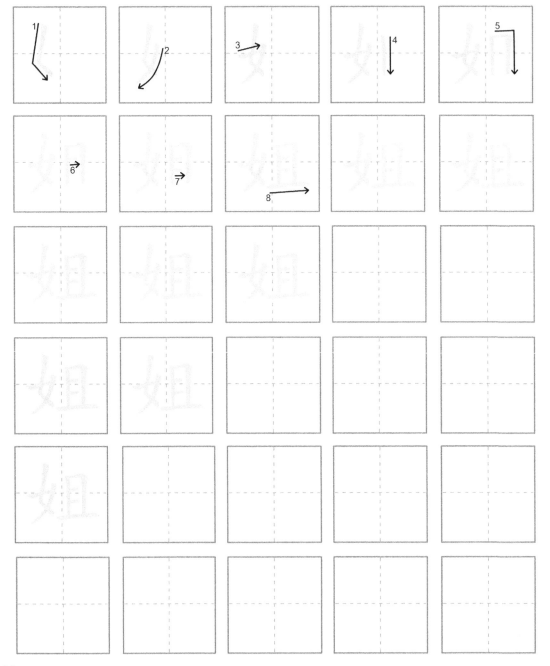

Let's Practice Writing

Find

Find the 姐姐 older sister that matches the example. Draw a circle around her.

Example

🐟 Trace and write the Chinese character 姐 (older sister).

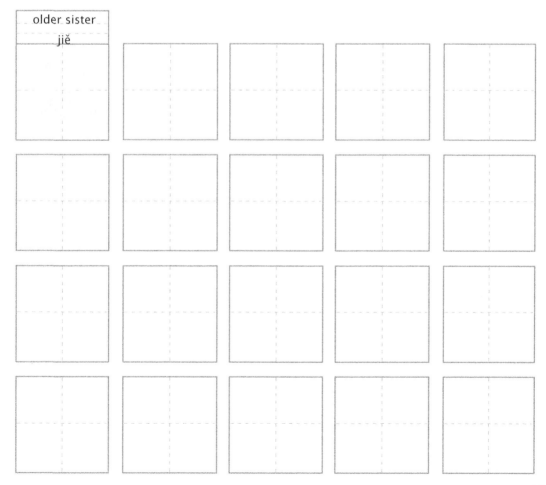

| older sister | | | | |
| jiě | | | | |

Let's Practice Writing

younger brother
dì
弟

弟弟
dìdì

Color

Color the picture and Chinese characters 弟弟 (younger brother).

Trace and write the Chinese character 弟 (younger brother).

Let's Practice Writing

Trace

Trace a path along the dashed lines from the picture of the younger brother to the Chinese character 弟.

弟

 Trace and write the Chinese character 弟 (younger brother).

younger brother dì				

Let's Practice Writing

younger sister
mèi
妹

mèimei

Color

Color the picture and Chinese characters 妹妹 (younger sister).

Trace and write the Chinese character 妹 (younger sister).

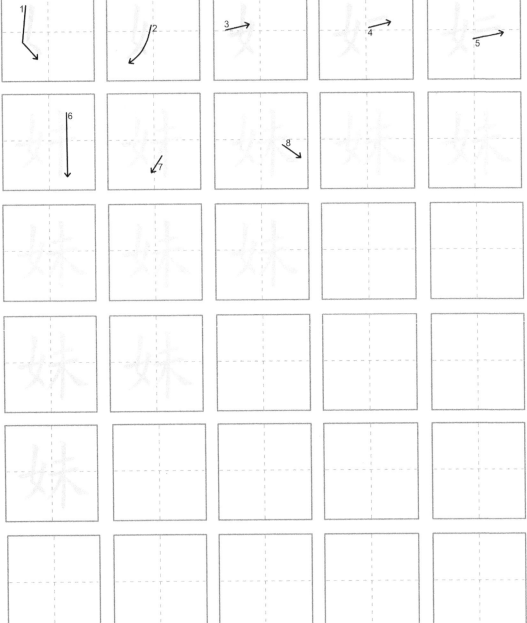

Let's Practice Writing

Find

Find the 妹妹 younger sister that matches the example.
Draw a circle around her.

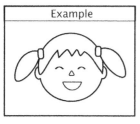
Example

Trace and write the Chinese character 妹 (younger sister).

younger sister mèi				

Let's Practice Writing

older uncle (dad's older brother) bó
伯

bóbo

Color

Color the picture and Chinese characters 伯伯 older uncle (dad's older brother).

Trace and write the Chinese character 伯 older uncle (dad's older brother).

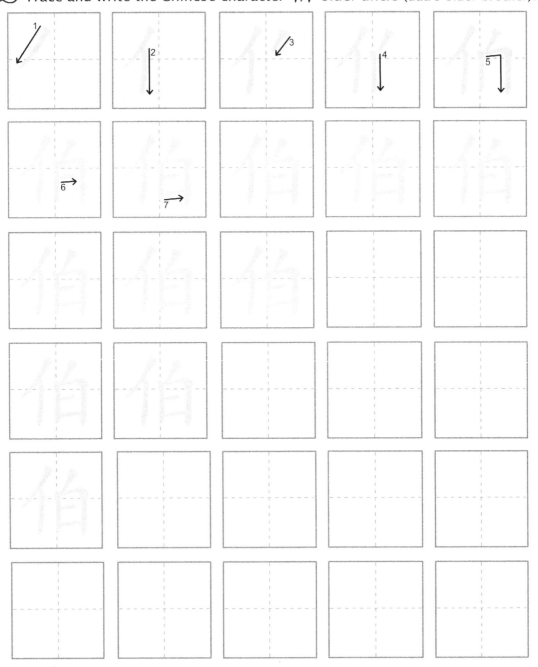

Let's Practice Writing

Different

Look at the two pictures of 伯伯 older uncle (dad's older brother). Circle the differences.

Trace and write the Chinese character 伯 older uncle (dad's older brother).

older uncle (dad's older brother) bó				

33

Let's Practice Writing

★★★

younger uncle
(dad's younger brother)
shū

叔

shūshu

Trace and write the Chinese character 叔 younger uncle (dad's younger brother).

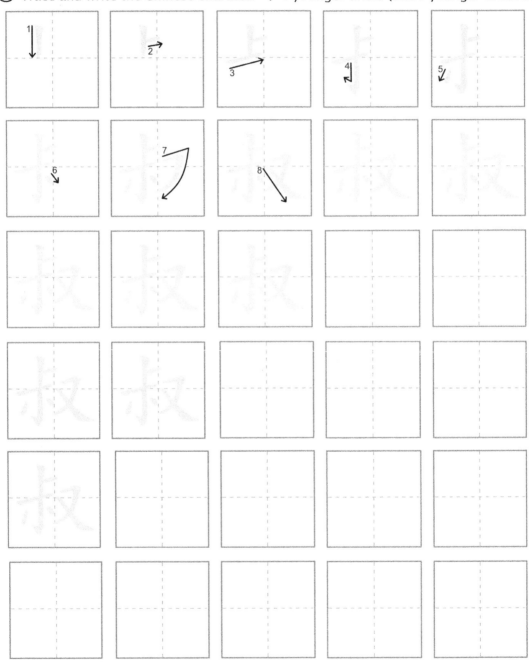

Let's Practice Writing

Different

Look at the two pictures of 叔叔 younger uncle (dad's younger brother). Circle the differences.

Trace and write the Chinese character 叔 younger uncle (dad's younger brother).

younger uncle (dad's younger brother) shū				

younger aunt (dad's younger sister) gū
姑

gūgū

Helpful Tip

When 姑 and 妈 are put together. They form the word 姑妈 older aunt (dad's older sister).

🐟 Trace and write the Chinese character 姑 younger aunt (dad's younger sister).

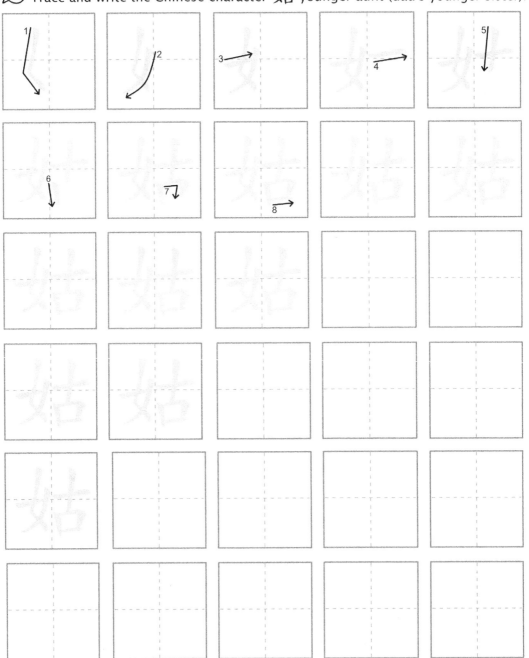

Let's Practice Writing

Pattern

Look at each row. What comes next? Circle the character 姑 or to complete the pattern.

 姑 姑   姑

 姑   姑   姑

ᗧ Trace and write the Chinese character 姑妈 older aunt (dad's older sister).

older aunt (dad's older sister)	
(dad's older sister) gū	mom mā

uncle (mom's brother) jiù
舅

jiùjiu

舅舅 is used for both older or younger uncle (mom's brother).

Trace and write the Chinese character 舅 uncle (mom's brother).

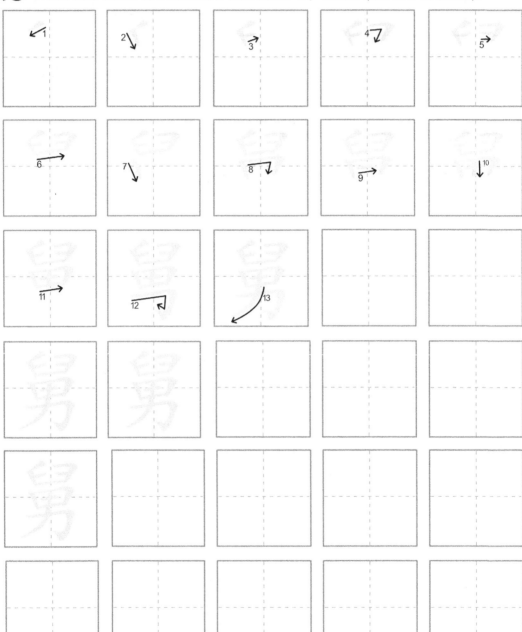

Let's Practice Writing

Draw

Look at the example. Finish drawing the face for uncle 舅舅 (mom's brother).

Example

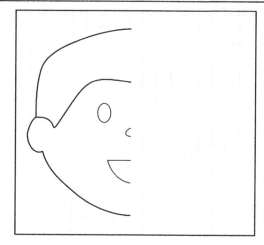

🐟 Trace and write the Chinese character 舅 uncle (mom's brother).

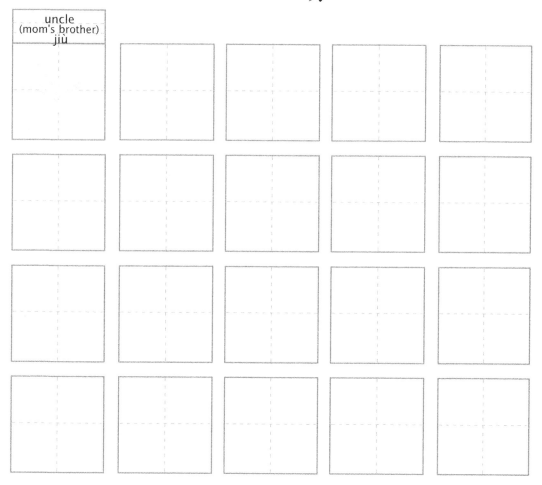

uncle (mom's brother) jiù				

aunt (mom's sister) yí
姨

姨妈

yímā

Helpful Tip

Add 姨 to 妈 for 姨妈 meaning "older aunt" on mom's side.

🐟 Trace and write the Chinese character 姨 aunt (mom's sister).

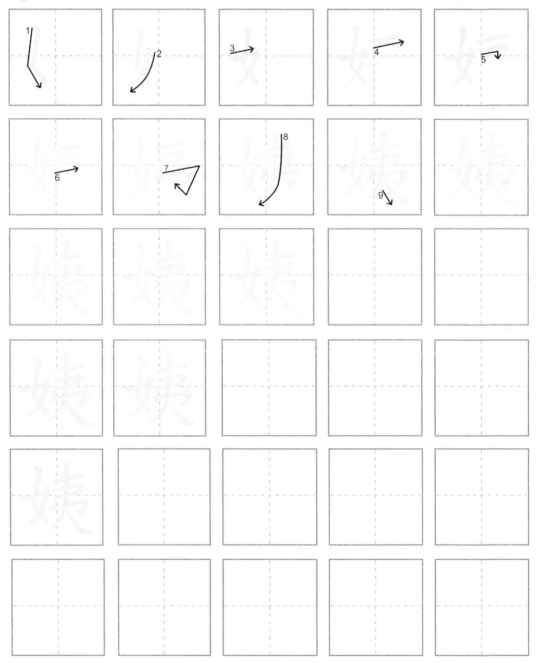

Let's Practice Writing

Draw

Draw a silly face on 姨 aunt (mom's sister).

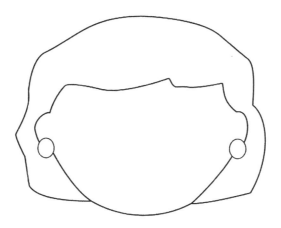

Trace and write the Chinese character 姨妈 aunt (mom's older sister).

older aunt (mom's older sister)	
aunt yí	mom mā

Let's Practice Writing

younger aunt (mom's younger sister)	
prefix for kinship ā	aunt yí
阿	姨

āyí

Helpful Tip

Add 阿 to 姨 for 阿姨 meaning "younger aunt" on mom's side.

Trace and write the Chinese character 阿 prefix for kinship.

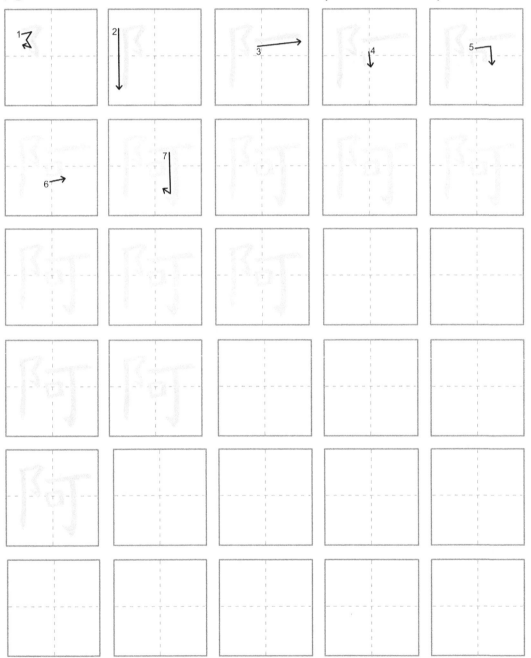

Let's Practice Writing

Draw

Draw more flowers on 阿姨 younger aunt's (mom's younger sister's) hair.

Trace and write the Chinese character 阿姨 younger aunt (mom's younger sister).

younger aunt (mom's younger sister)	
prefix for kinship ā	aunt yí

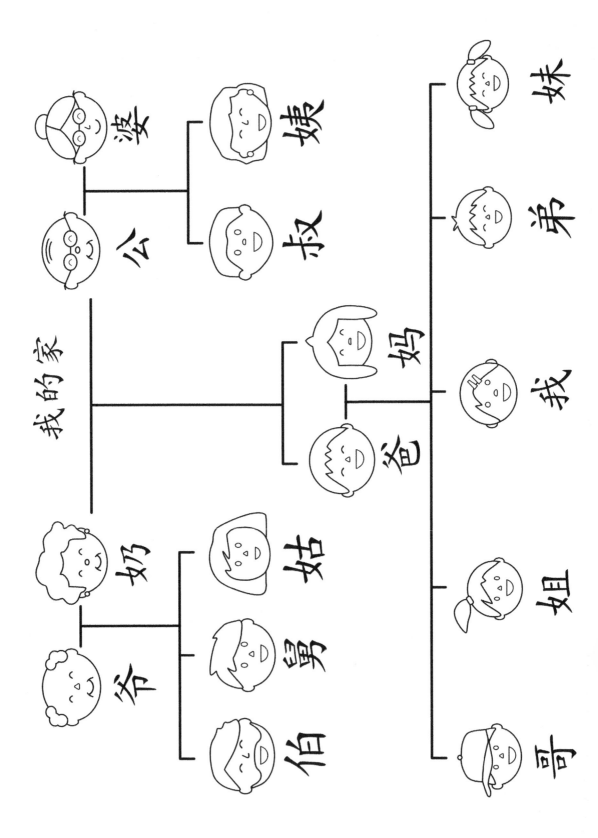

Let's See Your Family

Draw and Write

Draw the members of your family 家人 in the picture frames.
Write who they are in Chinese in the label under each picture.

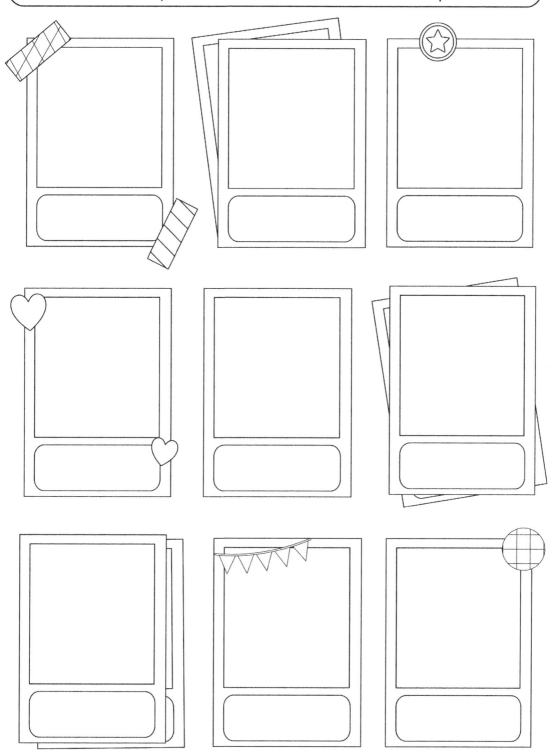

Let's Review

Match
Draw a line from each Chinese character to its meaning.

我　家　人　婆　奶

person　grandma (dad's mother)　I, me　family, home　grandma (mom's mother)

爸　爷　我的　公　妈

grandpa (dad's father)　my　dad　grandpa (mom's father)　mom

Let's Review

Match

Draw a line from each Chinese character to its meaning.

姑　弟　伯　叔　姐

older sister　older uncle (dad's older brother)　aunt (dad's sister)　younger uncle (dad's younger brother)　younger brother

哥　妹　姨　舅　的

older brother　uncle (mom's brother)　of　aunt (mom's sister)　younger sister

47

older male cousin (dad's sibling's son)	
paternal relation táng	elder brother xiōng
堂	兄

Helpful Tip

Add 堂 to 弟 younger brother, 姐 older sister and 妹 younger sister for more cousins (children of dad's siblings).

堂兄 = older male cousin   堂妹 = younger female cousin

堂弟 = younger male cousin

堂姐 = older female cousin

▷ Trace and write the Chinese character 堂 (paternal relation).

Let's Practice Writing

Word Search

Circle all the 堂兄 older male cousin (dad's sibling's older son).

堂	哥	妹	妹	姐	弟	堂	姐
兄	姐	弟	堂	兄	妹	兄	弟
妹	弟	堂	姐	弟	哥	哥	姐
弟	妹	哥	哥	堂	姐	妹	堂
姐	堂	兄	弟	兄	哥	妹	兄

Trace and write the Chinese character 堂 (paternal relation).

paternal relation				
táng				

Let's Practice Writing

★ ★ ★

older male cousin (dad's sibling's son)	
paternal relation táng	elder brother xiōng
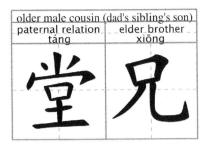	

Trace and write the Chinese character 兄 (elder brother).

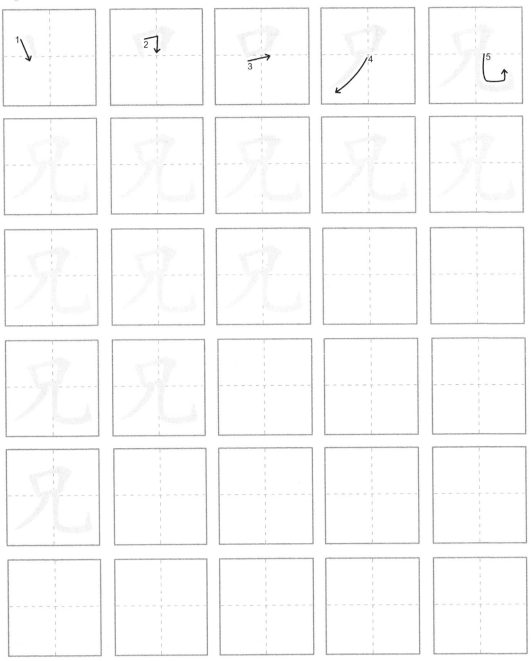

50

Let's Practice Writing

Puzzle

Circle the stroke to complete the word 堂兄 older male cousin (dad's sibling's older son).

 ➡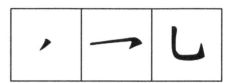

 ➡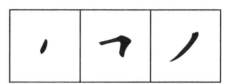

Trace and write the Chinese character 兄 (elder brother).

elder brother
xiōng

Let's Practice Writing

maternal relation
biǎo

Helpful Tip

Add 表 to 哥 (older brother), 弟 (younger brother), 姐 (older sister) and 妹 (younger sister) to create words for cousins (children of mom's siblings).

表哥 = older male cousin   表姐 = older female cousin

表弟 = younger male cousin   表妹 = younger female cousin

🐟 Trace and write the Chinese character 表 (maternal relation).

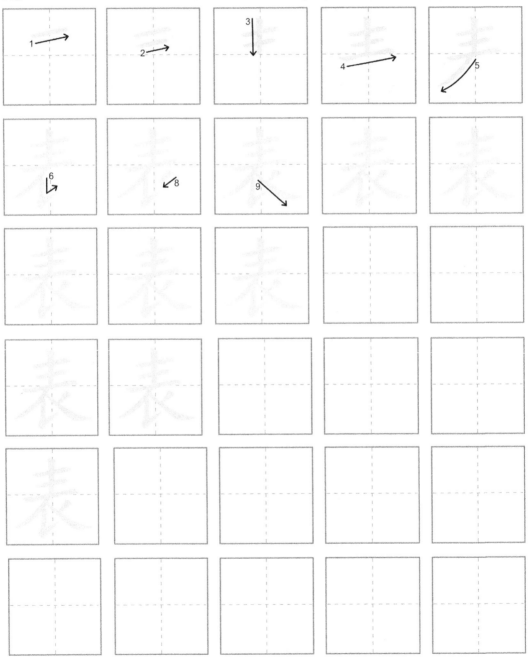

Let's Practice Writing

Match

Match the cousins with a 表 maternal relation (children of mom's siblings). Draw a line from each book to its name tag.

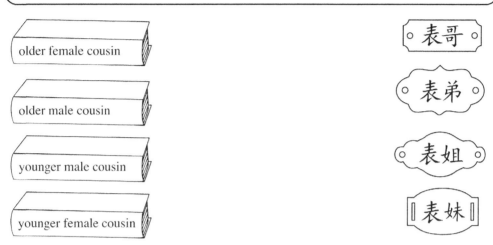

older female cousin

older male cousin

younger male cousin

younger female cousin

表哥

表弟

表姐

表妹

Trace and write the Chinese character 表 (maternal relation).

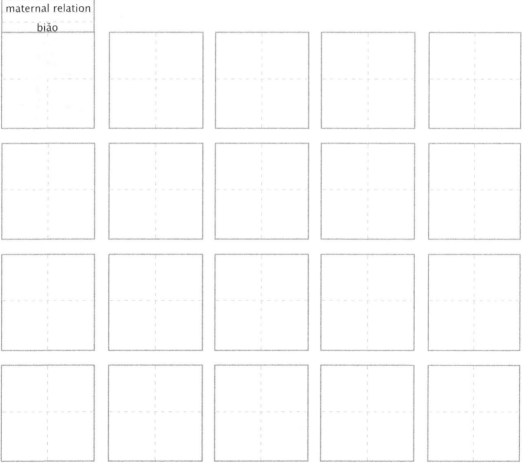

maternal relation
biǎo

★ ★ ★

pet	
to pamper, spoil chǒng	thing wù

Helpful Tip

When 宠 and 物 are put together, they form the word 宠物 meaning "pet".

🐟 Trace and write the Chinese character 宠 (to pamper, spoil).

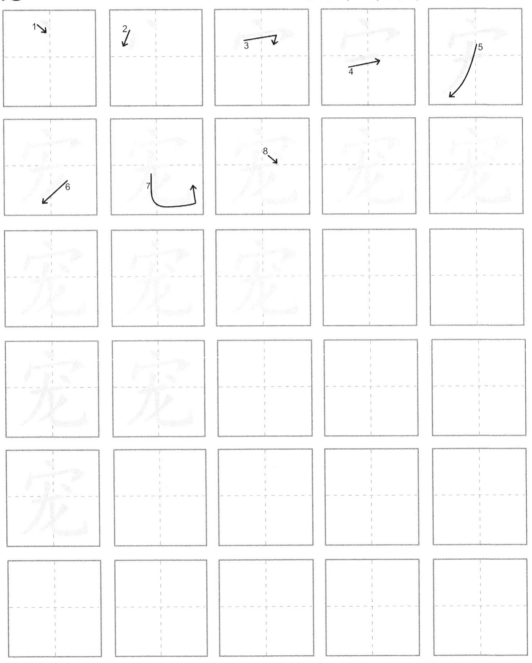

Let's Practice Writing

Draw

Draw your favorite 宠物 pet.

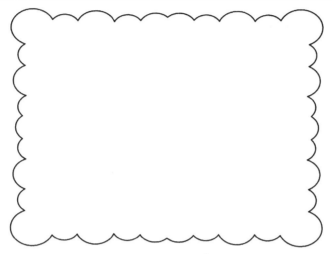

Trace and write the Chinese character 宠 (to pamper, spoil).

to pamper, spoil chǒng				

Let's Practice Writing

pet	
to pamper, spoil chǒng	thing wù
宠	物

Color

Color the characters 宠物 meaning "pet".

🐟 Trace and write the Chinese character 物 (thing).

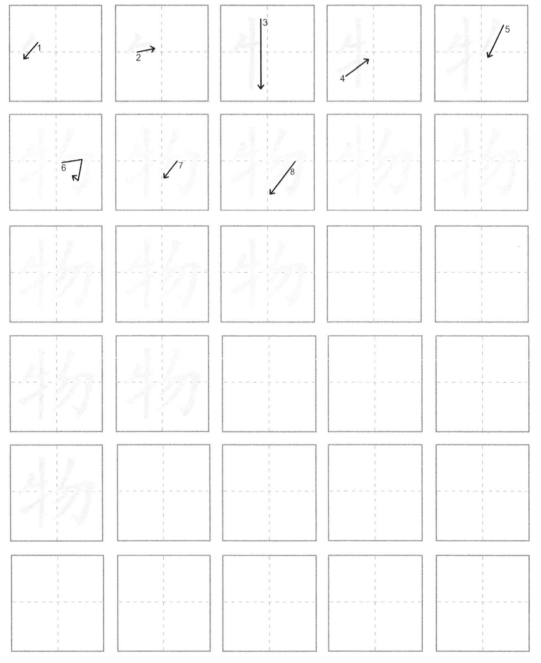

56

Let's Practice Writing

Maze

Start from the arrow at 宠 (to pamper, spoil) and draw a line to 物 (thing) to make the word 宠物 (pet).

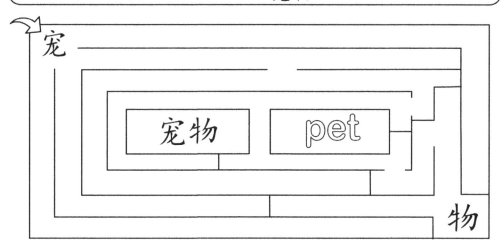

Trace and write the Chinese character 物 (thing).

thing				
wù				

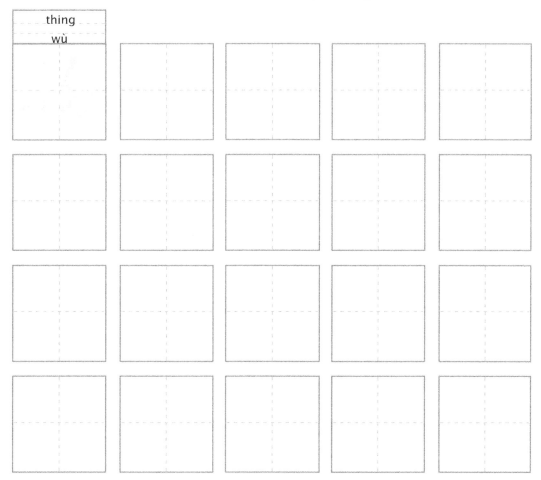

Let's Practice Writing

cat
māo

猫

猫

🐟 Trace and write the Chinese character 猫 (cat).

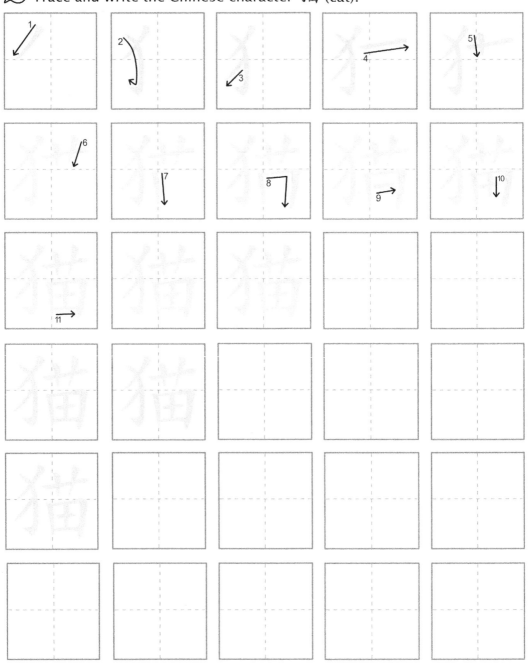

Let's Practice Writing

Maze

Start at the arrow and draw a line to the Chinese character 猫 (cat).

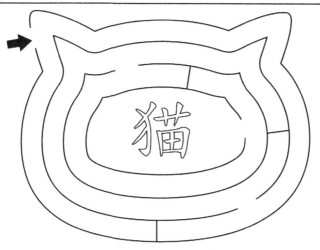

Trace and write the Chinese character 猫 (cat).

cat
māo

Let's Practice Writing

★★★

dog
gǒu

狗

Color

Color the character 狗 and picture for dog.

Trace and write the Chinese character 狗 (dog).

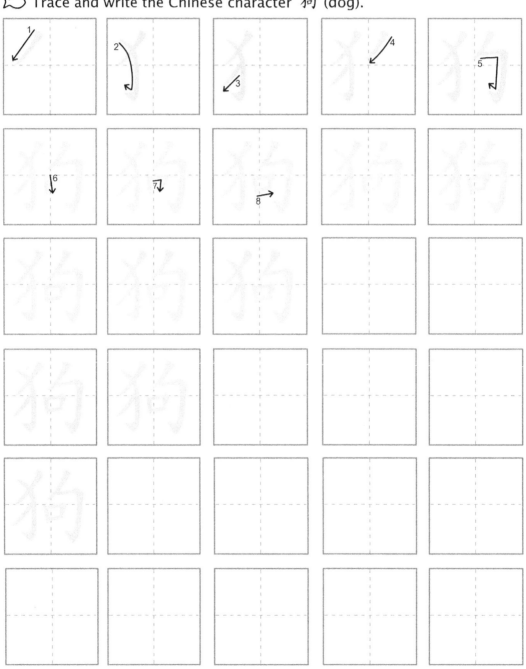

Let's Practice Writing

Analogy

Look at the top row. Circle the picture of the 狗 (dog) that goes best in the box on the bottom row with the question mark.

Trace and write the Chinese character 狗 (dog).

dog
gǒu

Let's Practice Writing

★ ★ ★

bird
niǎo
鸟

Color

Color the character 鸟 and picture for bird.

🐟 Trace and write the Chinese character 鸟 (bird).

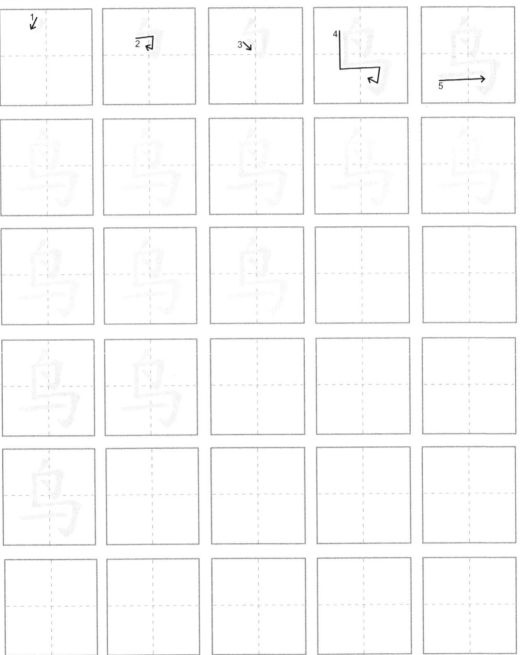

Let's Practice Writing

Reasoning

Look at the example. How many more worms are needed so each 鸟 bird has its own worm? Circle your answer.

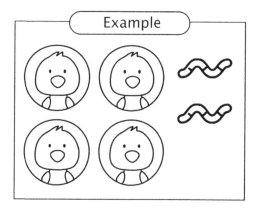

Trace and write the Chinese character 鸟 (bird).

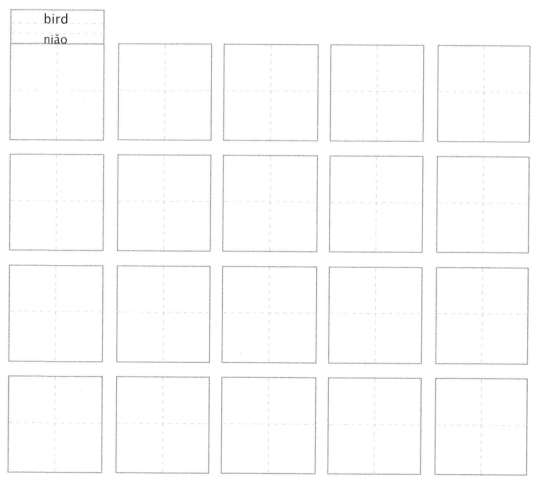

| bird |
| niǎo |

| fish |
| yú |

Color

Color the character 鱼 and picture for fish.

🐟 Trace and write the Chinese character 鱼 (fish).

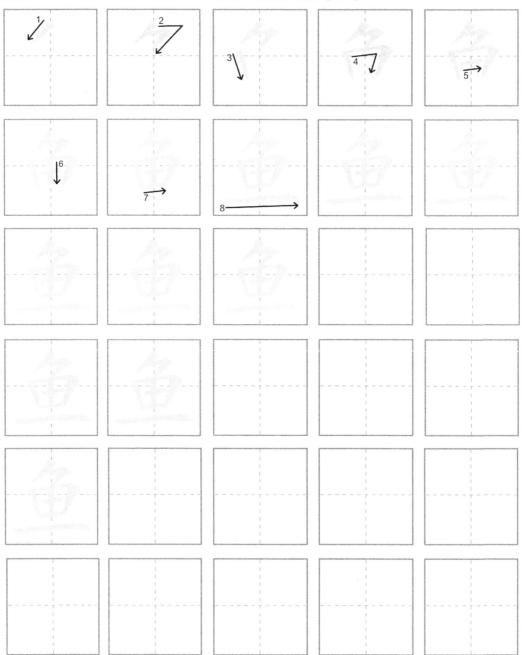

Let's Practice Writing

Different

Circle the differences in the 鱼 fish pictures.

Trace and write the Chinese character 鱼 (fish).

fish				
yú				

Match

Draw a line from each picture to its Chinese character.

宠物

狗

鱼

鸟

猫

Answer Key

Let's Check Our Answers

page 5

page 9

page 11

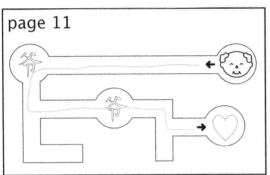

page 13

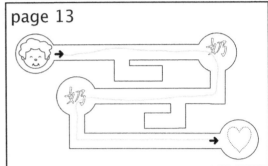

page 16

page 18

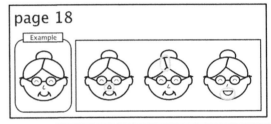

page 21

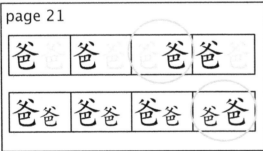

page 23

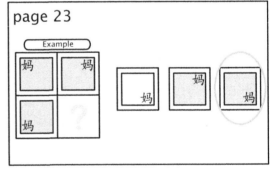

page 25

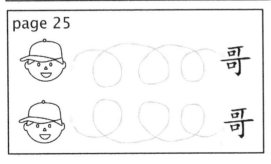

page 27

Let's Check Our Answers

page 29
弟

page 31

page 33

page 35

page 37
姑 姑 姑
姑 姑 姑

page 46
我 家 人 婆 奶
person | grandma (dad's mother) | I, me | family, home | grandma (mom's mother)

爸 爷 我的 公 妈
grandpa (dad's father) | my | dad | grandpa (mom's father) | mom

page 47
姑 弟 伯 叔 姐
older sister | older uncle (dad's older brother) | aunt (dad's sister) | younger uncle (dad's younger brother) | younger brother

哥 妹 姨 舅 的
older brother | uncle (mom's brother) | of | aunt (mom's sister) | younger sister

page 49
堂 哥 妹 妹 姐 弟 堂 姐
兄 姐 弟 堂 兄 妹 兄 弟
妹 弟 堂 姐 弟 哥 哥 姐
弟 妹 哥 哥 堂 姐 妹 堂
姐 堂 兄 弟 兄 哥 妹 兄

Let's Check Our Answers

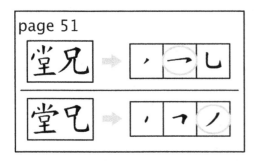

page 51

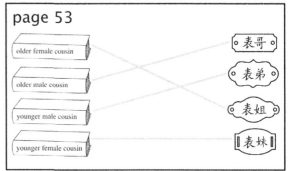

page 53

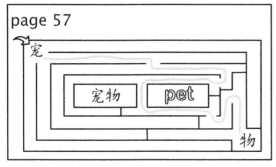

page 57

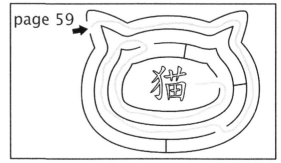

page 59

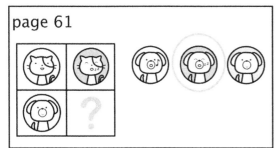

page 61

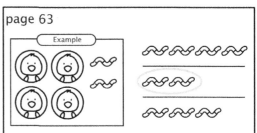

page 63

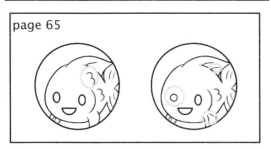

page 65

page 66

Good Job!

You have reached the end of **Chinese for Kids My Family Workbook Ages 5+ (Simplified)**.

Use this section to review and practice the Chinese characters you have learned. You will find:

- Coloring page
- Chinese character flashcards checklist
- Blank grid practice pages

Have fun learning!

Color

Color the Chinese characters for "my family".

Let's Review

I, me
wǒ

How to Use Flashcards

1) Cut out flashcards along the dashed lines.

2) Review flashcards at least twice a week to memorize words.

☐

my	
I, me wǒ	of de

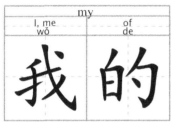

☐

grandma (dad's mother) nǎi

☐

family, home
jiā

☐

grandpa (mom's father)	
outside wài	husband's dad gōng

☐

person
rén

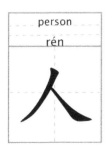

☐

grandma (mom's mother)	
outside wài	husband's mom pó

☐

Flashcards Checklist on Other Side

Let's Review

Flashcards Checklist

Check the box of each Chinese character you recognize.

dad	
bà	
爸	 ☐

younger brother	
dì	
弟	 ☐

mom	
mā	
妈	 ☐

younger sister	
mèi	
妹	 ☐

older brother	
gē	
哥	 ☐

older uncle (dad's older brother)	
bó	
伯	 ☐

older sister	
jiě	
姐	 ☐

younger uncle (dad's younger brother)	
shū	
叔	 ☐

Flashcards Checklist on Other Side

Let's Review

Flashcards Checklist

Check the box of each Chinese character you recognize.

aunt (dad's sister) gū

☐

grandpa (dad's father) yé

☐

uncle (mom's brother) jiù

☐

paternal relation táng

Children of dad's siblings

堂兄 = older male cousin
堂弟 = younger male cousin
堂姐 = older female cousin
堂妹 = younger female cousin

☐

aunt (mom's sister) yí

姨妈 = older aunt (mom's older sister)

☐

maternal relation biǎo

Children of mom's siblings

表哥 = older male cousin
表弟 = younger male cousin
表姐 = older female cousin
表妹 = younger female cousin

☐

younger aunt (mom's younger sister)	
prefix for kinship ā	aunt yí

☐

Flashcards Checklist on Other Side

Writing Paper

Name

Date

Practice writing the Chinese characters you have learned below.

Good Job!

Writing Paper

Name	Date

🐟 Practice writing the Chinese characters you have learned below.

Good Job!

Writing Paper

Name

Date

Practice writing the Chinese characters you have learned below.

Good Job!

Name	Date

Practice writing the Chinese characters you have learned below.

Good Job!

Writing Paper

Name

Date

Practice writing the Chinese characters you have learned below.

Good Job!

Writing Paper

Name	Date

Practice writing the Chinese characters you have learned below.

Good Job!

Writing Paper

Practice writing the Chinese characters you have learned below.

Good Job!

Writing Paper

Name	Date

🐟 Practice writing the Chinese characters you have learned below.

Good Job!

Writing Paper

Date

Practice writing the Chinese characters you have learned below.

Good Job!

Writing Paper

Name

Date

🐟 Practice writing the Chinese characters you have learned below.

Good Job!

Writing Paper

Name	Date

🐟 Practice writing the Chinese characters you have learned below.

Good Job!

Writing Paper

Date

Practice writing the Chinese characters you have learned below.

Good Job!

Writing Paper

🐟 Practice writing the Chinese characters you have learned below.

Good Job!

Writing Paper

★ ★ ★

| Name | Date |

🐟 Practice writing the Chinese characters you have learned below.

Good Job!

Writing Paper

Name	Date

🐟 Practice writing the Chinese characters you have learned below.

Good Job!

Name	Date

Practice writing the Chinese characters you have learned below.

Good Job!

Writing Paper

Practice writing the Chinese characters you have learned below.

Good Job!

Writing Paper

Practice writing the Chinese characters you have learned below.

Good Job!

Writing Paper

🐟 Practice writing the Chinese characters you have learned below.

Good Job!

Writing Paper

Name	Date

🐟 Practice writing the Chinese characters you have learned below.

Good Job!

Writing Paper

Practice writing the Chinese characters you have learned below.

Good Job!

Writing Paper

★ ★ ★

Name	Date

🐟 Practice writing the Chinese characters you have learned below.

Good Job!

Writing Paper

Name	Date

🐟 Practice writing the Chinese characters you have learned below.

Good Job!

Writing Paper

Name	Date

Practice writing the Chinese characters you have learned below.

Good Job!

Writing Paper

Practice writing the Chinese characters you have learned below.

Good Job!

Writing Paper

Name	Date

🐟 Practice writing the Chinese characters you have learned below.

Good Job!

More From Chinese For Kids

Made in the USA
Middletown, DE
16 October 2023

40881274R00060